The Bug Bus

by Carmel Reilly

illustrated by Pauline Reeves

T0342742

OXFORD
UNIVERSITY PRESS
AUSTRALIA & NEW ZEALAND

Bill ran to the big bus.

Bill got on.

The bus hit a lot of mud.

The bus can not go.

Bill gets off the bus.

Bill hits a lot of mud.

It is no fun.

Bill gets back on the bus.

11